Icky Animals! Small and Gross

Creepy Caterpillars

Celeste Bishop

PowerKiDS press.
New York

Published in 2016 by The Rosen Publishing Group, Inc.
29 East 21st Street, New York, NY 10010

First Edition

Editor: Sarah Machajewski
Book Design: Mickey Harmon

Photo Credits: Cover, pp. 1, 3–4, 7–8, 11–12, 15–16, 19–20, 23–24 (splatters) GreenBelka/Shutterstock.com; cover (caterpillars) Fabio Sacchi/Shutterstock.com; p. 5 graja/Shutterstock.com; p. 6 konmesa/Shutterstock.com; p. 9 Lukas Jonaitis/Shutterstock.com; p. 10 RidvanArda/Shutterstock.com; p. 13 (inset) PHOTO FUN/Shutterstock.com; p. 13 (main) chinahbzyg/Shutterstock.com; p. 14 azure/Shutterstock.com; p. 17 Cathy Keifer/Shutterstock.com; pp.18, 21, 22 (main) hwongcc/Shutterstock.com; p. 22 (moth) alslutsky/Shutterstock.com.

Library of Congress Publication Data

Bishop, Celeste, author.
Creepy caterpillars / Celeste Bishop.
pages cm. — (Icky animals! Small and gross)
Includes index.
ISBN 978-1-4994-0698-6 (pbk.)
ISBN 978-1-4994-0699-3 (6 pack)
ISBN 978-1-4994-0702-0 (library binding)
1. Caterpillars—Juvenile literature. I. Title. II. Series: Bishop, Celeste. Icky animals! Small and gross.
QL544.2.B478 2015
595.7813'92—dc23

2014048526

Manufactured in the United States of America

CPSIA Compliance Information: Batch #WS15PK: For Further Information contact Rosen Publishing, New York, New York at 1-800-237-9932

CONTENTS

What is this small and hairy bug? It's a caterpillar.

This bug's name may come from words that mean "hairy cat."

Caterpillars live in hot places. They also live in cool places.

Caterpillars can be many different colors.

Many animals like to eat caterpillars. They blend in with plants to stay safe.

Caterpillars eat leaves.
Eating helps caterpillars grow.

Caterpillars shed their **skin** as they grow. This means the old skin falls off their body.

SKIN

Caterpillars shed five times. Then, they form a hard covering around their body.

A caterpillar stays in the hard covering for days or weeks.

butterfly
moth

When the hard covering opens, the caterpillar is very different. It's now a **butterfly** or moth!

WORDS TO KNOW

butterfly

skin

INDEX

WEBSITES

Due to the changing nature of Internet links, PowerKids Press has developed an online list of websites related to the subject of this book. This site is updated regularly. Please use this link to access the list: www.powerkidslinks.com/icky/pllr